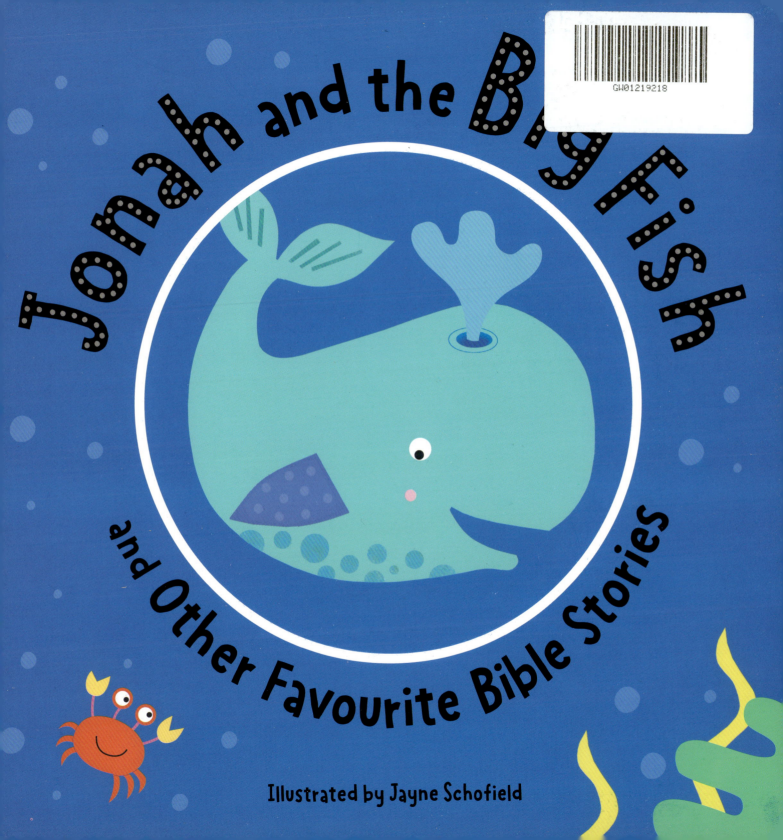

Jonah and the Big Fish

and Other Favourite Bible Stories

Illustrated by Jayne Schofield

GW01219218

Creation

God made all that you can see –
the sky, the Earth and a special tree.

Eden was a **beautiful** place, where Adam and Eve lived in God's **grace**.

But Adam and Eve **chose** their own way.
They ate **forbidden fruit** one day.

A crafty **serpent** tempted Eve, so she and Adam had to **leave.**

Noah and the Ark

God saw Noah was **faithful** and **good**,
so asked him to **build** an **ark** of **wood.**

Noah took **animals,** two by two, just as God had **told** him to do.

When Earth **flooded**, they stayed **afloat**, safe and dry aboard the **boat**.

Later, when the land was **dry**, God made a **rainbow** in the sky.

Joseph and the Dream Coat

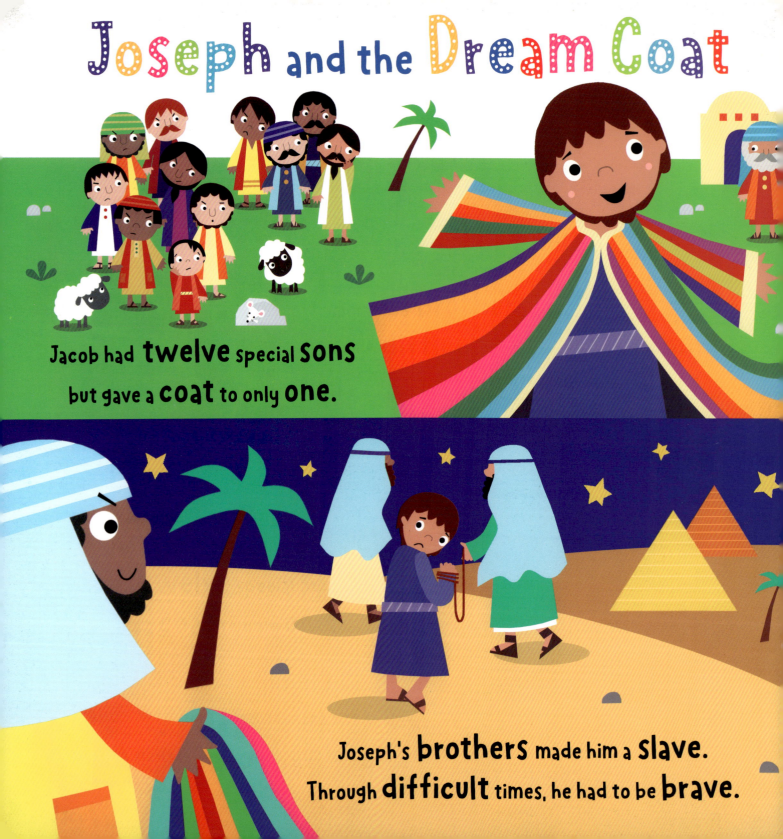

Jacob had **twelve** special **sons** but gave a **coat** to only **one**.

Joseph's **brothers** made him a **slave**. Through **difficult** times, he had to be **brave**.

Pharaoh's **dream** meant that **hunger** would come,
but Joseph's **plans** saved **everyone!**

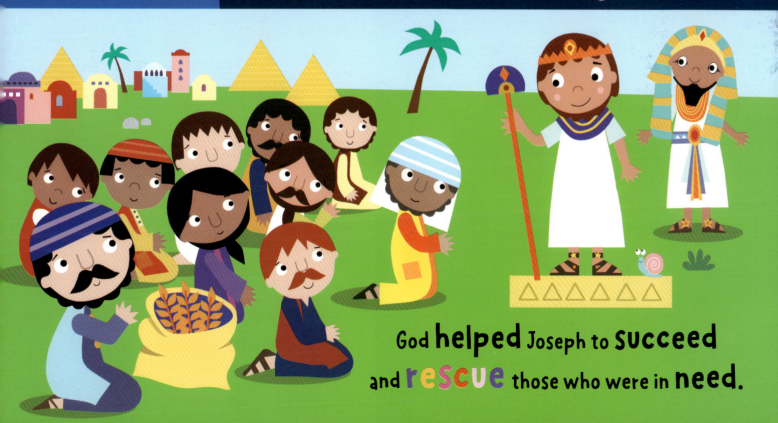

God **helped** Joseph to **succeed**
and **rescue** those who were in **need.**

Moses

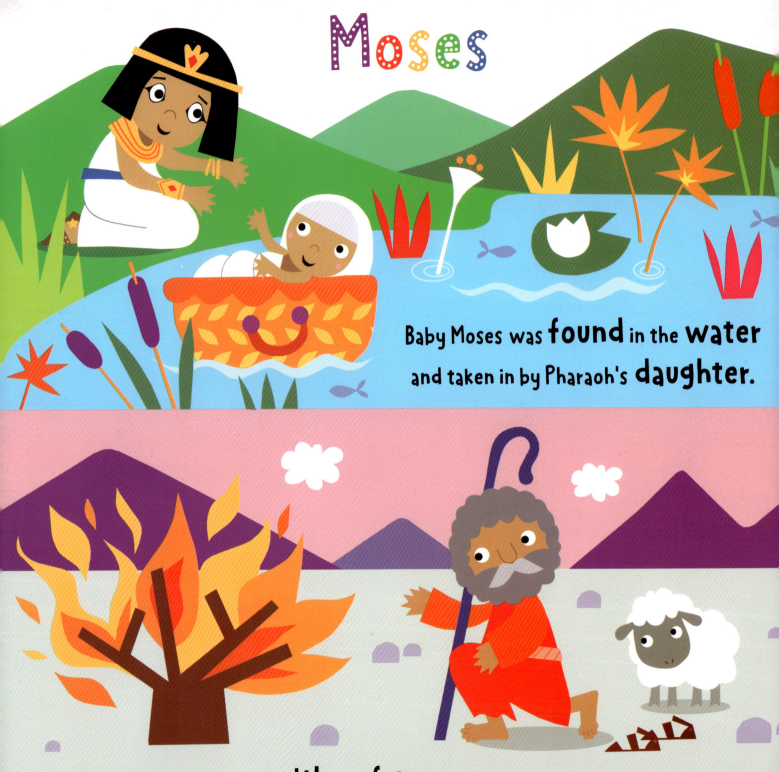

Baby Moses was **found** in the **water** and taken in by Pharaoh's **daughter**.

Then Moses left his **wealth** and **fame** to go and work in God's great name.

Pharaoh brushed aside God's warning,
so a new plague came each morning.

God helped Moses part the sea
and set the Israelite people free.

David and Goliath

A **war** broke out against King Saul,
led by a **giant**, so **broad** and **tall**.

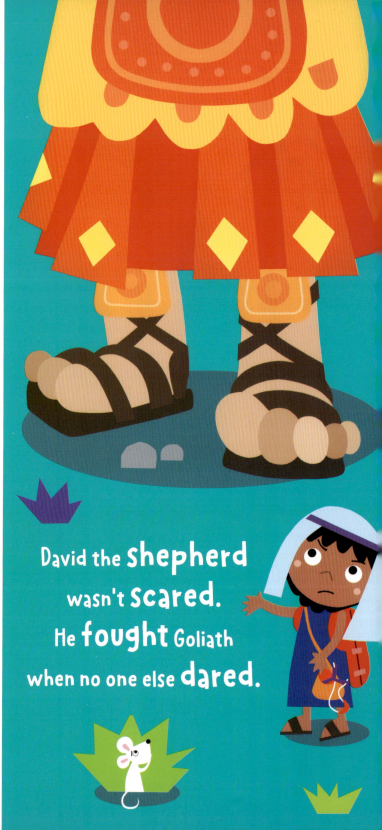

David the **shepherd**
wasn't **scared**.
He **fought** Goliath
when no one else **dared**.

Brave young David threw a stone.
Goliath fell down with a groan!

God helped David win the fight,
proving that faith is stronger than might.

Daniel and the Lions

Daniel was **trusted** by the **king**, so he **took care** of everything.

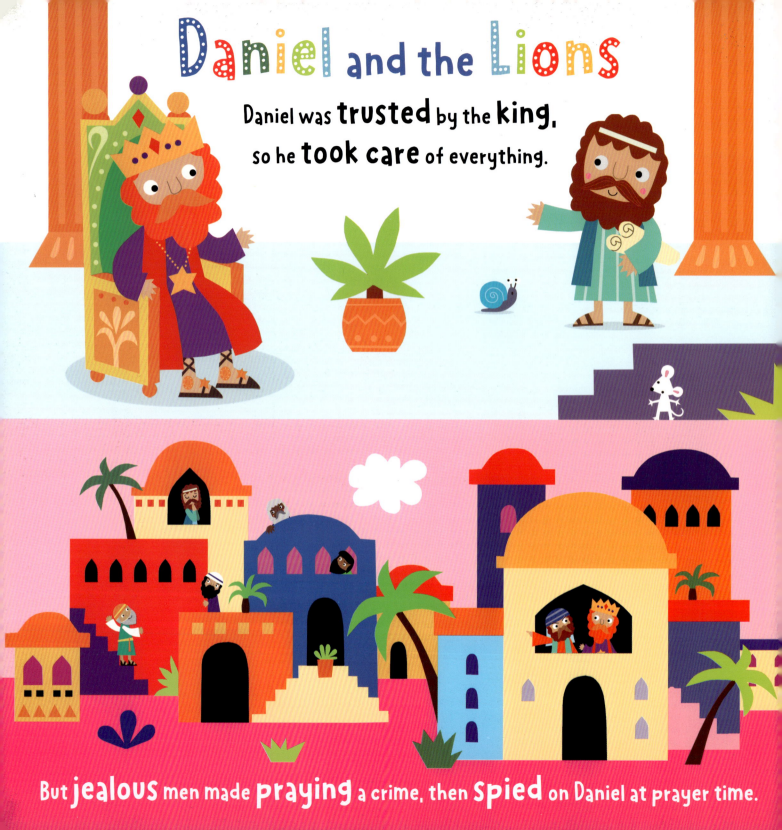

But **jealous** men made **praying** a crime, then **spied** on Daniel at prayer time.

They **threw** him in a **lions' den**, because his prayers had **angered** them.

But there was no need for **alarm** – God kept Daniel **safe** from harm.

Jonah and the Big Fish

God told Jonah about his **plan**, but Jonah turned away and **ran**.

Nineveh

Escape to sea

He boarded a **boat** to take a **trip**.

A huge **storm** threw him off the ship.

But God made sure he didn't **drown.**

A **big fish** gulped poor Jonah down!

After **three** days **praying** at sea,

God told the fish to set him **free.**

The Nativity

An angel told Mary she'd give **birth**
to a **son** who'd save the **Earth**.

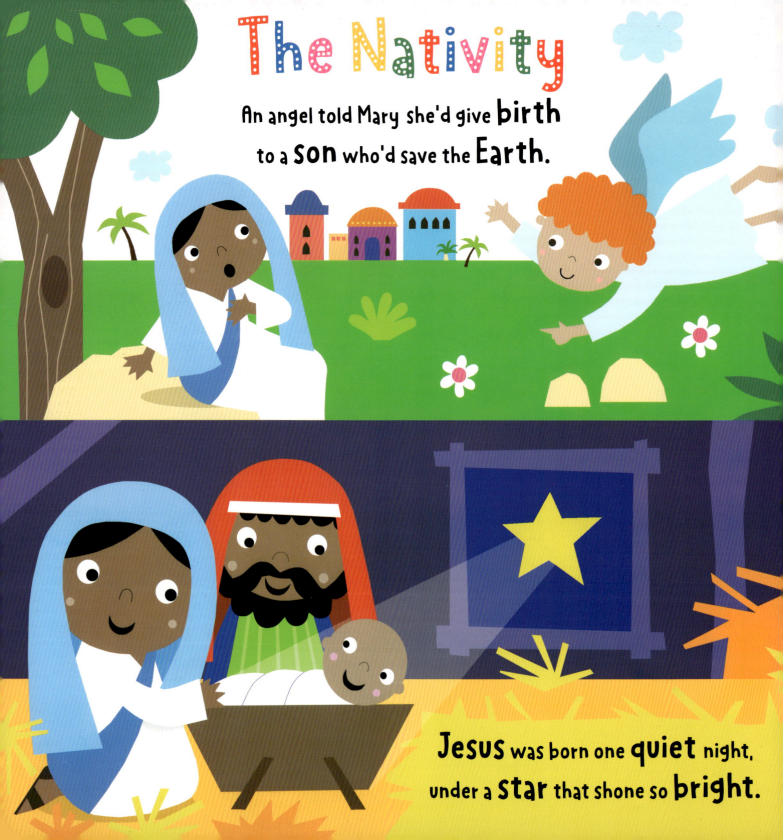

Jesus was born one **quiet** night,
under a **star** that shone so **bright**.

Some shepherds quickly spread the news:

Today is born the King of Jews!

Wise men came from far to see the Son of God, and this was He!

Feeding of the 5,000

Five thousand people came one day
to hear what Jesus had to say.

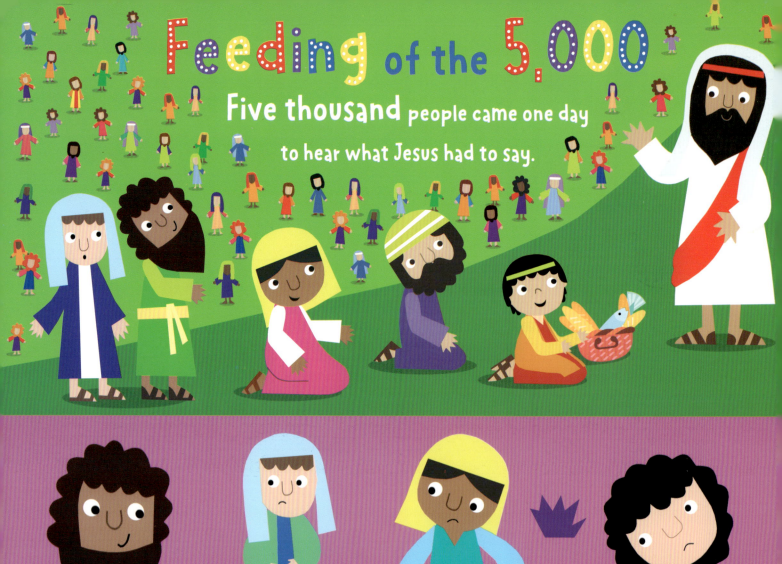

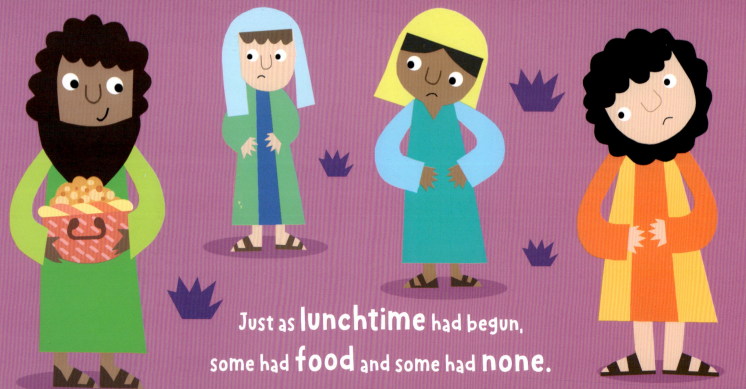

Just as **lunchtime** had begun,
some had **food** and some had **none**.

One small boy had **fish** and **bread,**

and with just this,
the crowd was **fed!**

Everyone ate, and still there was **more!**
They gathered **twelve baskets** of crumbs from the floor.

The Good Samaritan

Here's a **story** Jesus told – a man was **robbed** of **clothes** and **gold**.

Two men passed and heard him yelp, but neither of them stopped to **help**.

A **Samaritan** was walking by
and came as soon as he heard the **cry.**

Jesus wants us to **help** when we can, like the **kind** Samaritan man.

Easter

Jesus went from **town** to **town**
to spread God's **message** all around.

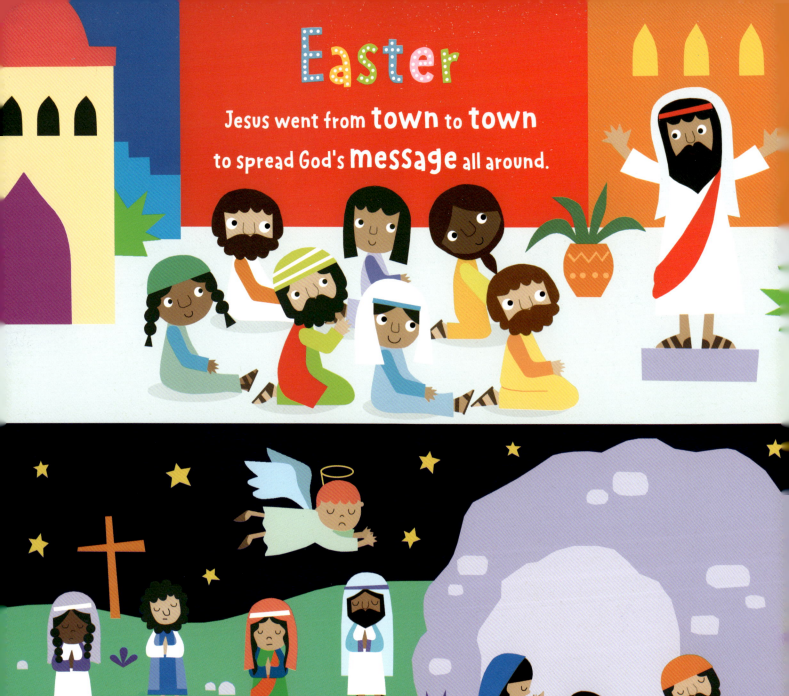

Then Jesus **died** and went to the **grave**
for us – the ones He came to **save**.

Three days later,
the tomb was bare.

Jesus' body
was not there!

Jesus had risen to life once more, and that is what we praise Him for.